Stress Less
and Thrive!

Resolving Work Stress, Relationship Stress and Post Traumatic Stress.

By

Craig Cox PhD

2021

Table of Contents

INTRODUCTION

My intention to simplify stress and stress management was in danger of spiralling out of control!

I struggled to balance the scientific theory with practical application and to keep things real. I find that in life it is very easy to get lost in the nice feeling of it all and not use that feeling to delve into the depths of ourselves.

Few people fail to realise what a big impact stress has on our lives. It is not just soldiers and first responders who are exposed to extremes or who have stress issues.

The crux of the matter is that our subconscious mind does not differentiate between real and imagined events. If we watch a movie that involves extreme killing and violence, we respond in our subconscious mind as if we are there!

I have found it difficult to get a definitive and practical answer to stress related questions. Both professionals and lay persons always seem to have a vague response that involves the words adrenaline, fight or flight, mindfulness and relaxation.

No one that I have engaged with so far has been able to explain to me what stress is, why we have it, why we respond in the way we do, what the stress triggers are, why they work and how we can practically and effectively manage our stress.

In this book I will;

Define stress in simple terms.

Empower the reader to understand the context of their stress.

Explore basic physiology of stress there by giving the reader an understanding of the chemical hormonal responses in the body.

Show how the metaphysical concepts of perception and awareness impacts on our world experience and how we can take charge of this self perpetuating feedback cycle.

Explain practical techniques to manage every day stress and Post Traumatic Stress.

Each one of us has our own unique experience of stress based on, and triggered by our personal perceptions of our world in relation to the perceived problems that we are confronted with.

No one experiences stress in the same way - the stress reaction is the most unique personal experience a person will have. The same group of people experiences quite different internal responses to apparently identical external experience.

The way we choose to define stress, the way we choose to react or respond to stress, and how we manage or control our stress is all dependent on and governed by a person's unique perceptions of themselves in their environment and their unique perceptions of others and their engagement of the world around them.

In the modern world of instant reporting, go-pro cams and drones, we are actually there in the action on our TV or computer screens!

We then have high pressure jobs, lack of job security, environmental concerns, political concerns, social changes and everything else from traffic to cell phones that impact on our lives physically and subconsciously. No one teaches us to cope with these events and the ensuing emotions.

I feel that if a person, either a normal person experiencing stress or a counsellor were to read my book and take out the pieces that they need and apply the techniques to their clients' needs and circumstances a positive change in the approach to life will be achieved and the purpose of this book will have been fulfilled.

I specifically explain in detail the mechanism of stress and the physiological pathway in terms that people can understand. Many stress seminars that I have attended have either erred on the side or being overly clinical and psychological or overly flippant and juvenile.

Not one seminar or book that I have read has linked motor co-ordination, writing and poetry as a way to engage our logical and emotional responses and as such I feel the simplicity of this process lends its self to everyone who is willing to make positive changes in their lives.

It is also simple enough to adapt the process to group sessions for post traumatic stress and emotional stress sufferers.

The methods and understanding outlined in this book combined with clinical intervention and detailed psychological intervention where appropriate is an unbeatable system to maintain our stress levels and optimize our experiences.

A weak point of this system is that is it time and effort intensive. Results will come with persistent work and intervention, and in a world where time is a scarce commodity people may not want to commit the resources to completing the system.

There is no way to half do this. A cursory read through the book' will start to activate the subconscious mind to start the stress management and healing process, but this may not be enough for some people.

The system also requires the use of old fashioned technology, a pen and paper. Every result in life is directly proportional to the effort and energy expended to achieve that result. I do hope people persist with the systems outlined here and heal and grow.

Whichever way I look at stress, the immediate intervention solution always comes back to the two basic fundamentals of perception and awareness. By listing simple intervention tricks and techniques that I have used in my life I hope to create an immediate shift in awareness in the reader. A small shift in awareness goes a long way to alleviating stress and preventing stressful situations.

Chapter One

Basic Principles of Stress

The first person to describe the body's reaction to stress was Walter Canon. This was in 1915. He laid the groundwork for the modern meaning of stress by describing the "fight or flight response" as a "series of biochemical changes that prepare you to deal with threats or danger". (https://en.wikipedia.org).

Canon acknowledged that organisms under stress "needed quick bursts of energy to fight or flee predators. In modern society however social custom prevents you from fighting or running away and so this emergency response is rarely allowed.

The emotional aspect of this response is a constant influence on us and can accumulate and cause unstable emotional outbursts such as road rage, depression and post traumatic stress disorder." (Cox 24)

The Four Stress Components

The four simple stress components that I identified are;

1. Stress is a UNIQUE experience. What makes you stressed may not make another person stressed.

2. A person's stress is directly related to their AWARENESS and PERCEPTION of their environment.

3. The trigger that activates the stress reaction is a brain frequency threshold of around 25 Hz (Beta brain wave function)

4. The brain does not subconsciously distinguish between what you physically see and experience in the world, and what you imagine. Both of these "events" are seen as external input and treated in exactly the same way." (Cox 14-15)

General Adaptation Syndrome

"Hans Selye, the first major Researcher on stress, was able to trace exactly what happens in the body during the stress response. He introduced the term General Adaptation Syndrome (GAS) to describe this" (https://www.stress.org/about/hans-selye-birth-of-stress)

The basic fundamentals of GAS are as follows;

Alarm Reaction

The first step is the alarm reaction. This allows us to cope in extreme situations or emergencies. It was found that any stimuli

– real or imagined, activated the cerebral cortex and the resulting message sent to the hypothalamus activated the sympathetic nervous system. This is the start of the stress reaction, the symptoms of which are;

Increased heart rate, cold extremities, increases in muscle tension and blood pressure, the diaphragm locks causing the person to breathe shallowly, the digestive system is interrupted and in severe cases the person will throw up and void their bowels. Resources are being routed to the brain, heart and large muscles so we can respond physically and violently if necessary. There are long term negative effects of this.

These hormones are specifically designed to boost our performance and reduce our response to injury. This alarm reaction response is perfect when escaping or fighting a threat, but extremely harmful when they are continuously in the body as they inhibit tissue repair, digestion, reproduction and cell division.

The inhibitions are necessary in the short term, but are very destructive if continuous over long periods of time. The accelerate ageing and exacerbate disease. This is the "Primitive" stress reaction.

Resistance Reaction

The Resistance Reaction phase is the result of prolonged stress. When the body is under continued pressure, the body begins to break down protein to fuel the response, and the metabolism and blood pressure are maintained at elevated levels.

Continued elevated levels of Cortisol, Adrenalin and other stress related hormones are experienced. This is what Cox terms the "Modern Stress" reaction.

Exhaustion

The final and most dangerous phase of GAS is the state of exhaustion. In this exhaustion phase the body has either depleted its available resources and con no longer respond effectively, or the body is unable to utilise the available resource. The result is that the body either succumbs to the stressor or an extreme disease occurs in the body such as cancer, coronary disease, depression, addictive behaviours and suicide.

In our fast paced society, with its multitude of stress inducing events, many persons remain in the resistance stage of the GAS almost continuously.

Glucocorticoids are helpful, they reduce inflammation and help us manage pain but they are very detrimental in the long term - they inhibit the normal immune responses, making the body more susceptible to infection and disease. Some common diseases linked to this GAS exhaustion phase are ulcers, high blood pressure, atherosclerosis and arthritis.

Types of Stress

The most fundamentally important definition of stress is;

A point in time when a person's perceived ability to cope is challenged by perceived events that they are experiencing in their environment.

Psychology has identified both positive and negative stress and has many subcategories such as nor-stress and U-stress. All of these categories are important in the realm of psychotherapy and other therapies, but we are reducing stress down to much more simple components.

I have simplified this to highlight two basic types of stress – Primitive stress and modern stress.

Imagine you are walking peacefully in your local park. You look up and see a huge Sabre toothed cat bearing down on you.

What do you do?

You would probably drop everything and run away!

That is a primitive stress reaction – we do whatever we have to do to survive. This reaction is not normally needed for longer than 10 minutes.

This reaction is perfect - we survive.

Primitive Stress

Primitive stress is a short intense emotional and physical state that is necessary to combat an immediate threat in order to survive. Subconsciously there is a positive result every time that the response occurs - he organism is still alive!

Primitive stress is pure survival instinct. It is short, sharp and intense and then is resolved. This is where we find the clichéd "fight or flight" response. If one considers this carefully the fight or flight response is actually a secondary response. The primary responses will be feint or freeze.

The Feint and freeze response seems to have been developed specifically to counter the threat of large feline predators.

While studying archaeology and anthropology in the early 1990's we observed a behavioural adaptation experiment where a baboon unexpectedly encounters a snake close to it. The baboon would immediately feint. After a short period of time the baboon would wake up and run away chattering warning others of the danger.

Either evolution or some other survival resource has taught the baboon and even human beings that if one is not a threat to the snake, it will not bite. Similarly the cliché of a lady feinting when encountering a mouse had to originate somewhere and it is common for people to feint when they see their own bold or the blood of others!

Similarly if a human encounters a large predator like a lion or a tiger, the first response will be to freeze. The primary predators of humans and other primates are the big cats. Cats will only attack something that is moving so if the animal, primate or hominid just freezes, it has a very good chance of surviving long enough to assess the situation and then decide to either fight or flight.

It is well documented how the Masai peoples of Kenya and the San peoples of the Kalahari will chase lions from their kill and take meat from the carcass. When they are leaving and are attacked by the lions, they will fall flat on the ground and play dead. The lion will then pounce on the marauders, sniff around and leave!

Immobility in most stressful situations is the primary life saving response, there after the secondary fight or flight will activate.

After this initial response we enter into our secondary response, the well known fight or flight mode.

Problems arise when we think about this stressful situation for the next twenty to fifty years!

This we can categorise as modern stress.

The constant thought process is part of how we cope with stress and adapt our behaviour to survive, but it is also the major contributing factor to our modern stress. The nature of this imaginary event reaction is accumulative and can be very damaging to our well being.

Modern stress

Modern stress is a form of long term constant emotional pressure to perform in a specific way with constant negative judgements being derived from comparing performance to expectation. This encompass bot the Resistance and Exhaustion phase of GAS.

Modern stress usually involves prolonged low intensity stress inputs that do not resolve themselves over time or after the stress event is over. A typical modern lifestyle involves long commute times, pressure to be on time, pressure to perform, achieve targets, dealing with other people issues in situations where people have very little control.

There is a constant demand for our attention, for our time and constant pressure to achieve and not fail. Very rarely in the modern world do we need our stress response to function as designed – as in facing a predator.

This constant low intensity pressure is the problem that most people face.

How often do people get to their client or office and shout for joy because they made it there and are still alive?

How often do people reach their goal or target only to have more work and more pressure handed to them?

It seems that the human stress response is not the problem, but the society and systems within which we need to function are the problem!

This is exacerbated by the practicality of our existence – we cannot all just go and live in the bush or on a mountain – it is neither practical nor is it desirable.

Our ability to cope will be called into question whenever our perceived demands threaten to outweigh our perceived resources. We will experience some type of stress whenever our ability to cope is challenged or threatened in some way.

When our ability to cope collapses, then so does, our self-acceptance, self-worth and our self-esteem.

Cox observed that this is common and is a direct result of "Modern Stress". The process seems to be that we experience and respond in the primitive stress reaction, survive, but then perceive ourselves to be a failure. This perceived failure occurs when we compare ourselves to our peers and the expectation that we think society has of us and our behaviour and achievements.

Extreme cases of this can cause a confabulation in our subconscious mind and lead to split personalities, depression, psychosis and other severe identity and psychological issues.

Most people in today's society experience primitive stress in sporting events – both participants and spectators, and first responders. Watching TV and news channels and movies triggers this primitive stress response. (Cox 18)

"Chronic or modern stress can occur when the stressors of life are unrelenting, as they are during a major reorganization or downsizing at work, living in financial debt or while undergoing a messy divorce or coping with a chronic or life threatening illness.

Chronic or modern stress also occurs when little stressors accumulate and you are unable to recuperate from properly them. As long as the mind perceives a threat, the body remains aroused. If the stress response remains turned on you can be increasing your chances of experiencing a stress related disease." Cox 18)

Motor coordination

Motor coordination can over-rule the stress response. If one sees the brains processing simplistically, we can deduce that it takes a lot of processing power to co-ordinate movement. This takes up valuable resources that could otherwise have been devoted to over thinking and speeding the brain up potentially reaching your stress trigger threshold. Motor co-ordination is also repetitive – walking or running or lifting weights in the gym requires vast amounts of attention and co ordination with very little analytical reasoning.

The worries and overly analytical thoughts that are essential for stress have to take second place because the body is now in motion and needs to remain in motion safely.

From a primitive stress perspective, the primary responses of feinting or freezing are types of motor co-ordination. Then the secondary stress responses of fighting or running away take over and these are also motor co-ordination responses.

The act of engaging motor coordination in the present stressful situation serves to regulate the response and reduces the response and processes some of the stress hormones almost immediately.

In a primitive world, one cannot run away from a predator and have a panic attack at the same time. Running away and surviving takes precedence, then when we have survived and are safe, we go into what most modern people would class as stress – running through all the what if, should have, could have scenarios in our thoughts!

In the modern world and for the purpose of this stress awareness system, Motor coordination is used extensively. To do this we need to write.

Writing with a pen on a piece of paper or a diary is a series of incredibly complex motor coordination actions. It involves the understanding and processing of language, syntax and the nuances of culture as well as very fine and precise motor coordination actions all carried out over an extended period of time. This is very complex, and because motor coordination takes precedence over our stress response, the act of journal-ling or keeping a physical written diary will effectively stop and possibly reverse the stress response at that moment. Writing will also stop the memory accumulation cycle and allow us to find context and re-frame the stress events or issues that we need to re-frame.

Stress and Dis-Ease

Research into the relationship between stress and disease shows
that people with stress related disorders exhibit hyperactivity in
a particular system unique to that individual, either skeletal,
muscular, cardiovascular or gastrointestinal systems being the
most common areas. Some people will experience fatigue and
muscle tension, others migraine headaches, ulcers or
constipation and diarrhoea. Symptomatic diagnosis of chronic
stress is very difficult as each individual and circumstance is
different. (Cox 18)

"Almost every system in your body can be damaged by stress.
Suppression of the reproductive system can cause amenorrhoea
(cessation of menstruation) and failure to ovulate in women,
impotence in men and loss of libido in both. Stress-triggered
changes in the lungs increase the symptoms of asthma,
bronchitis, and other respiratory conditions. The constant
depletion of insulin during the stress response may be a factor in
the onset of adult diabetes.

Modern stress suspends tissue repair and remodelling. It causes
de-calcification of bones leading to osteoporosis and or
susceptibility to fractures. Inhibition of immune and
inflammatory systems makes you more susceptible to colds and

flu and can exacerbate some diseases such as cancer and AIDS (Acquired Immune Deficiency Syndrome). In addition, a prolonged stress response can worsen conditions such as arthritis, chronic pain and diabetes. There is also some evidence that the continued release and depletion of norepinephrine during a state of chronic stress can contribute to depression." (Cox 18 – 19)

The relationship between stress, disease, and ageing it also important to understand. Cox highlights "the changing patterns of disease and the emergence of degenerative disorders. Over just a few generations, the threat of infectious diseases such as typhoid, pneumonia, and polio have been replaced with such "modern plagues" as cardiovascular disease, cancer, arthritis, respiratory disorders such as asthma and emphysema, and a pervasive incidence of depression. As we age normally our physiology does change, but with a constant imbalance in the body's optimal stress levels, the body tends to grow old very quickly as a direct result of certain vital physiological structures and systems either shutting down or under-performing." (Cox 19)

Chapter Two

Perception, Awareness and the World

If we consider the important definition of stress - A point in time when a person's perceived ability to cope is challenged by perceived events that they are experiencing in their environment. We see the need to explore and define the concepts presented it in depth.

Dictionary definitions of the three fundamental components of stress are;

Perceive– 1. To become aware of (something) through the senses; recognize or observe. 2. To come to comprehend; grasp. (Collins English Dictionary 626)

Aware– 1. Having knowledge. 2. Informed

World– 7.an area, sphere or realm considered as a complete environment. 8. A state of existence. 9. The total circumstances and experience of an individual that make up his life. (Collins English Dictionary 48)

The famous Eastern philosopher, Osho, says that Awareness is what makes you a master. He means that awareness is what makes you who you are and if one has awareness, one automatically creates the world and the perception there of!

A simple illustration of this in his book "awareness" is if you are walking and are carrying stones that you think are diamonds, you will take great care of them and hold on tightly to them because of their perceived value in your world. As soon as you examine them and become aware that they are not diamonds, you reject them and throw them away because of the perceived lack of value in the world. Further, you can never again think that those stones or ones like them are diamonds!

We cannot unlearn or unknown something.

The human thought and reasoning process is very simple and follows this simply cycle

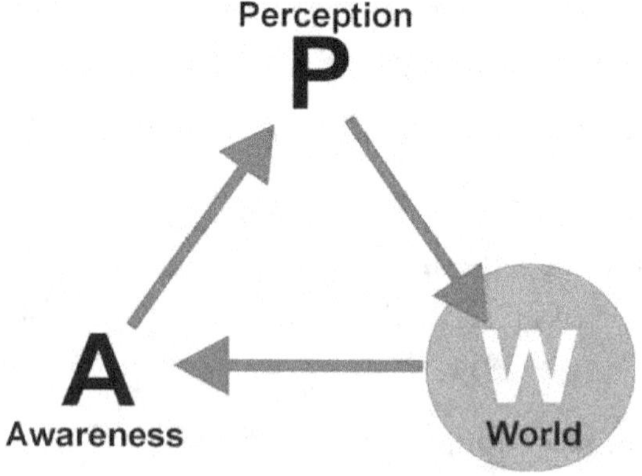

"As a person perceives (P) themselves in the world, they have a certain awareness (A) of themselves in that world (W). That

awareness then feeds back into your perception which causes them to make certain changes in the world. After these changes have been made, they have a fresh awareness of their new position in the world. This awareness then feeds into their perception and the whole cycle repeats again." (Cox 15)

An interesting metaphysical observation is that none of the three components can exist without the other two – even the world cannot exist without our perception and awareness of it. I discussed in my Master's thesis, now a book on meditation and manifestation, how matter follows thought and as such the very world that we are responding to is a result of our thoughts and those thoughts are tailored by our perception and awareness.

This is how humans learn and how they interact in the world. Once a person has gone round this cycle, they cannot erase the memory of what they have experienced and understood in that simple Perception – Awareness – World cycle. This cycle becomes part of your memory and part of who we are and how we define ourselves. This cycle cannot stop and seems to operate on a physical, soul and spiritual level or dimension.

Ian McFadyen combines perception and awareness and calls the combination World Pictures. He and his researches "were often struck by how differently other people see things. Sometimes it is as if they lived in a separate universe. However, generally, we do not believe that the universe is actually different for different people. What we assume is that people see the world differently.

We all have different World Pictures… Challenging someone's World Pictures may result in outright hostility or violence as many scientists and social reformers have discovered over the years when they tried to promote concepts such as a spherical earth, evolution, relativity, the unconscious mind and racial equality." (Mc Fadyen 15)

Chapter Three

The Stress Trigger

The fool proof un-hackable stress trigger is brain speed

"The human brain is a highly complex organ. Not even the most intricate computer begins to rival the complexity of the human brain. A soft, wrinkled mass of tissue weighing about 1.4 kilograms, the human brain is the most complex organ in the human body. Each of its 25 billion neurons is functionally connected to as many as 1000 others." (Cox 20)

What we do know is that at any moment millions of messages are flashing through the brain which is transmitting "decisions" back to the organs maintaining the appropriate heart rate, blood pressure, respiration rate, temperature, muscle tone and blood chemistry, at the same time receiving and responding to, hundreds of external messages such as hearing a ringing telephone, smelling a steak dinner, seeing the printed words on this page.

"Short term memory is essentially synonymous with the allocation of attention, and a prime function of short term memory is to concentrate on processing important aspects of the environment" (Cohen 65) It stands to reason that if more data is received than there is the available facility to process that information we will go into stress.

All the time that the brain is thinking and analysing, it is using up Nero-chemicals to transmit impulses from one neuron to another This creates a magnetic electrical activity which can be measured.

Brain Wave Frequencies

Continuous electrical activity within the brain can be measured by placing electrodes on the surface of the scalp and recording differences in electrical potentials. Patterns of activity called brain waves can be traced, producing a record called an electroencephalogram (EEG)

Brain waves are evoked primarily from the cerebral cortex, but some result from input from pathways projected through the thalamus. The rhythms arise from synchronized cyclic activity of groups of neurons. One's EEG is as unique as one's fingerprints, but the EEG changes with the state of consciousness or emotion. Often brain waves are irregular, but under some conditions distinct patterns can be recorded. One can also use a MRI scan for this!

Four main kinds of wave rhythms have been distinguished:

The Alpha wave rhythm , is evoked when a person is relaxed and resting with eyes closed. (6 Hz – 12 Hz)

Beta waves (14.0-30 Hz) are associated with concentration, arousal, alertness, and cognition but also anxiety, unease, fight and flight" (Stress & Brain Waves Sat, 2009-10-31 16:06 — Cheryl http://americannutritionassociation.org/node/257)

Delta waves are associated with normal sleep

Theta waves occur under emotional stress - especially frustration or disappointment.

A measurable (usually measured with an EEG – electroencephalogram or MRI – magnetic resonance Imaging scan) brain speed of around 25Hz will automatically trigger a physical stress response in the human body.

Anything at all, a real event, imagined event or remembered event that causes the brain to function above the 25Hz trigger automatically triggers a stress response.

The more data your brain has to process, the faster it will function and the more resources or capacity it will use. When the brain reaches a point where the available processing capacity is reaching its limit, the human organism automatically starts to regulate its self.

To perform this regulation efficiently more resources are made available to the organism so that it can physically remove its self quickly and efficiently from the environment in which it is that is currently causing the brain or processing centre of that organism to function close to its capability.

The human organism is designed to survive.

A fool proof way of doing this is to have a manually operated stress trigger that will activate under any circumstance that induces stress on that organism.

An interesting observation of brain wave activity and attention is how humans interact with modern entertainment – social media, movies and the predominance of screen based entertainment.

The primary motivation of entertainment is to find an external source of stimulus that will excite viewers or participants to a certain extent and maintain that excitement.

A hobby or mode of entertainment that is "boring" will not hold a person's attention and they will move on to something else. It seems that the positive aspects of stress are utilised by the movie makers and distributors to provide both relaxation for the viewers and make money. Screen entertainment seems to be designed specifically to keep the viewer on their 25Hz or higher stress trigger!

Chapter Four

Memory Theory

Memory seems to be a contentious area of psychological study. It seems very easy, we all remember things and we can trigger memories in ourselves and others with sounds, words, fragrances, tastes – any tactile input from our external and internal sensory world triggers memory recall and experience. We presume that this is real because we experience it, but if one has to give evidence in court about a third party incident, how real and reliable is it really?

To what do we compare these memories to calibrate them and how can one person's memory be more or less correct than another person's memory. It seems that memory is directly responsible for our perception and awareness and how we see ourselves in the world which as we have seen is the only contributing factor to our stress.

Schema Theory

The most logical theory of memory for the purposes of understanding our perception, world and awareness stress cycle was introduced in 1932 by a researcher called Bartlett. Bartlett proposed that the reason people tend to omit and re-structure aspects of stories that they are relating to a third party is because the information is assimilated into the story tellers own knowledge and experiences.

This developed into Schema Theory. "Schema theory emphasizes the fact that what we remember is influenced by what we already know… Schemas are packets of information stored in memory representing general knowledge about objects, situations, events or actions."(Cohen 25)

There are five basic characteristics of Schemas as proposed by Rumelhart and Norman (Cohen 25)

- Schemas encapsulate knowledge of all kinds

 - Schemas can be linked together into related systems and can have limited life spans.

- Schemas have compulsory information requirements to complete them for example a dog needs the following information requirements; four legs, teeth, hair, and tail.

- All different kinds of knowledge are incorporated – almost like a library index filing system that automatically cross correlates it's self

- Schemas can actively engage and interpret new inputs and self adjust, if one sees a three legged dog, the schema automatically updates its self.

These schemas are vital for our interactive processing and our resulting memory accumulation.

As already mentioned, we receive information from two sources – our internal world and our external world. We do not immediately judge the source of the information but rather react to it first then layer into the information our past experience.

Memory Accumulation

The stress reaction is not necessarily triggered by physical events alone. Stress can be triggered by memory. If a person thinks about a previous stressful event, the memory of that event will cause them to imagine that they are experiencing that event again, and they will have a physical stress reaction to that imaginary input.

In our modern stressful environment the majority of our stress is a result of us thinking about previous stress and then re living the physical reaction to deal with the event!

Time Progression

It is interesting to observe that as time progresses we subconsciously continue to re live our confrontations and stresses. According to Schema Theory discussed above, this is how we order ourselves in our world. What we do not realize is that every time we think about a stressful event, we first think about the previous thought we had about that event.

The previous thoughts are called memory traces and these "memory traces form the basic unit of representation in theories of episodic memory." (Cohen107) The memory traces act like old fashioned filing cards in a library, or the index on a file system on a pc. When activated they retrieve all of the data in the file and we then reference or encode these memories again from our current situation and experience.

We then react physically to the thought of the event first, then progress to the thought previous to that. We subconsciously re-live each associated event in reverse order and we apply the present moment's interpretation to that event there by creating an extra slightly altered event.

Look at the spiral diagram. Take the spiral to be time. The stress full event is in the centre. Every time we stop and look back at the event, we look through the previous thoughts of that event.

We react physically to those thoughts first, and then move on to the next thought.

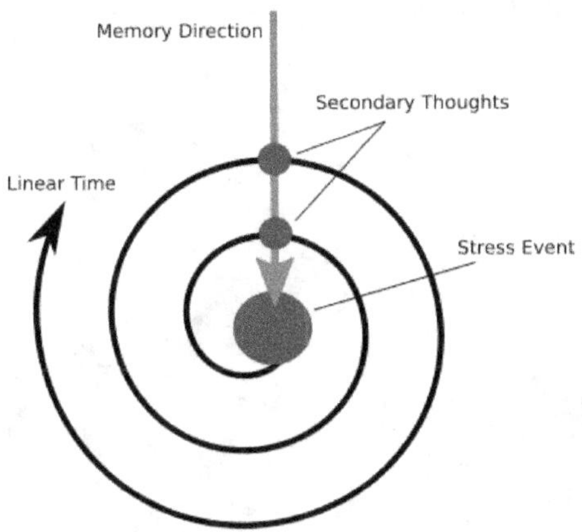

The physical reaction then cements that thought into our current experience of that thought. You then move on to the previous thought of the previous thought of the event, adding current value and current reactions at every level.

The process continues until you consciously understand the initial event and re frame it into something less stressful. This is similar to the analytical age regression technique developed by Milton Erickson.

In the following diagram you can see how the imaginary event (E) flips into the physical for the reaction. The reaction is then consolidated and becomes part of our memory.

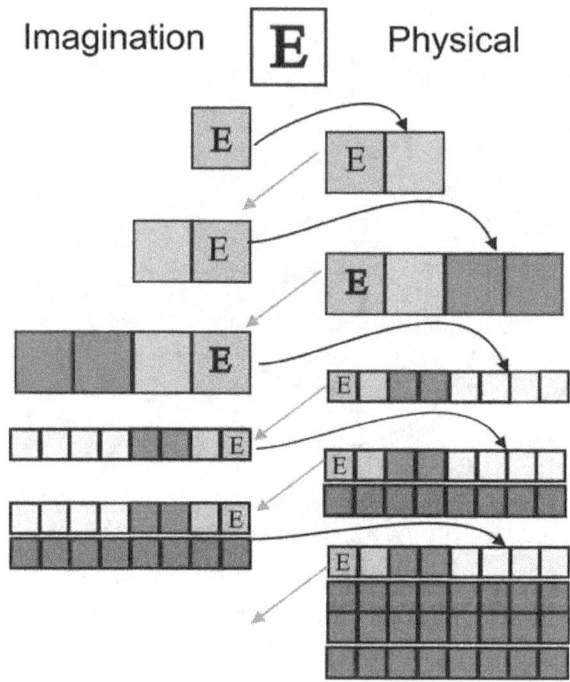

This consolidated reaction is placed on the imagination side as a consolidated unit. When you think about the event again, the current thoughts as well as all the accumulated previous thoughts are flipped over into the physical for the reaction.

Memory Accumulation has a Compounding Effect

This memory accumulation has a compounding effect and greatly enhances the severity of your stress reaction. Two things are important to remember here.

> **Firstly** it is important to remember that stress and our physical reaction is NOT necessarily linked to logic or reason. Stress is a primitive physical response to an event or circumstance, real or imagined.

> **Secondly** one must remember that the stress trigger is a brain speed of around 25Hz. As these memories compound the brain has to function faster and faster to deal with the ever increasing amount of data that is presented to it in a single moment. As soon as the brain goes past the 25Hz trigger we automatically enter into a physical stress response.

To effectively manage our stress, we need to slow the brain down and switch off our stress trigger. To do this we will use motor coordination which will be discussed in the Effectively Managing Stress chapter.

Chapter Five

The Physiological Stress Pathway

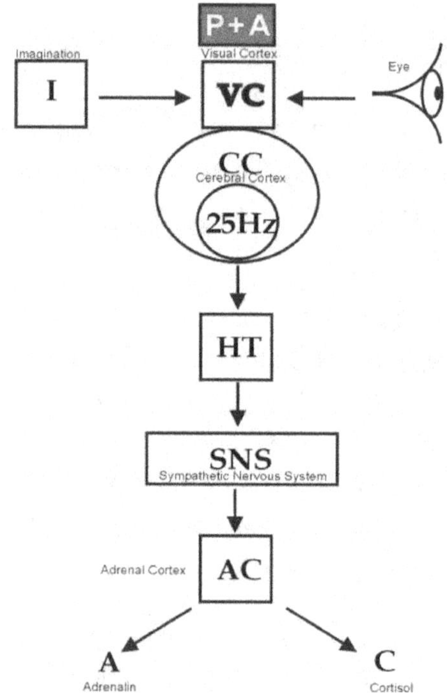

The Physiological pathway explained

The brain and neural pathways are incredibly complex. Add to this logic, reasoning, memory, spirituality and emotion and you can see just how complicated our stress response can be. To understand things better I have dramatically simplified the process. We do not need extra complicated clutter when we are delving into our stress!

Imagine your brain as your own personal hard drive. Just like your PC hard drive, the part of your brain that triggers your stress reaction, receives data, packages it for processing and sends it on to another part of your brain (the software in your PC) that analyses the data.

It does not make critical judgements.

Your hard drive does not distinguish between data received from the mouse, the virus, the CD drive, the internet etc. In the same way, the part of your brain that manages your stress does not care where the data comes from; it receives it, packages it and sends it on.

Data Inputs
We receive data from two places;

> **The first** is from our physical senses. Any place outside of our mind. This represents "the world out there". The majority of our primitive stress occurs here.

> **The second** is from our imagination. This is where the majority of our modern stress comes from.

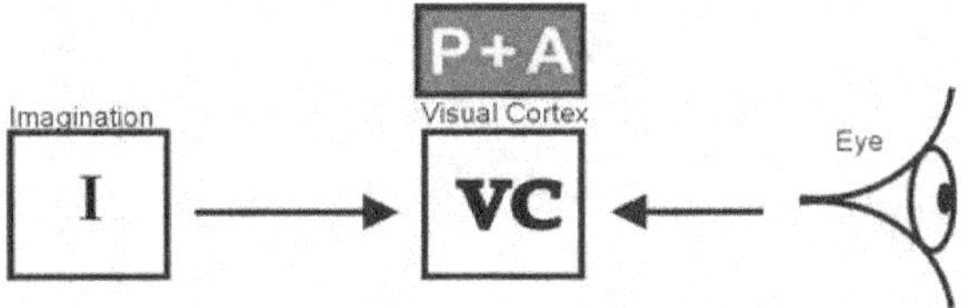

Both sets of data or inputs are received by the visual cortex. At this point there is no logical differentiation between where this data is coming from – real and imagined events are treated in the same manner.

The 25Hz Stress Trigger

Something needs to set the physical stress pathway in motion. This is a physical trigger that uses the speed at which your brain is functioning to gauge weather our survival is under threat or not.

"The trigger that activates the stress reaction is a brain frequency threshold of around 25 Hz (Beta brain wave function). (Cox 28)

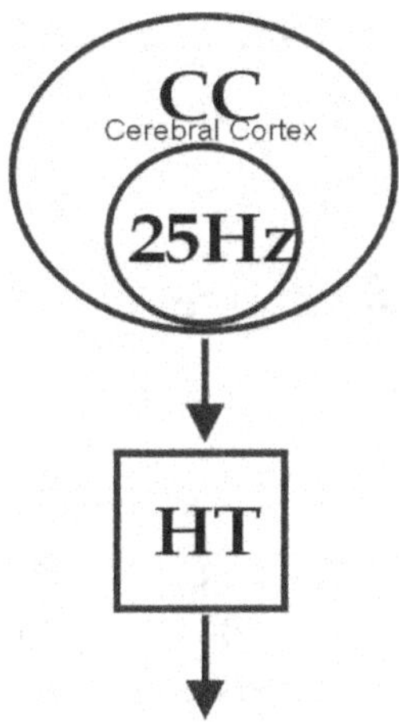

When your brain goes faster than the trigger (25Hz) we automatically go into a physical stress reaction. It is important to understand that ANYTHING – real or imagined that causes our brains to function fast and trip our trigger will cause us to go into stress.

The first thing to be activated in your stress reaction is your Hypothalamus. This is at the top of your brain stem. It is sometimes called your "Reptile brain". It is not very smart, and controls basic survival and body maintenance functions like your heart beat and breathing rhythm. You can see this as your command and control centre. If an intruder is in your house, you call the armed response company or the police. It is your hypothalamus that will answer that call and co ordinate the

release of resources so that you can face the threat, real or
imagined, effectively.

Sympathetic Nervous System

Your hypothalamus, your command and control centre then
activates' your Sympathetic nervous System. It is called your
sympathetic nervous System because it is sympathetic to
perceived events in our environment. It is separate from our
parasympathetic nervous system and is specifically designed to
interact with external factors.

You can imagine your sympathetic nervous system as being
your task force, SWAT team or fast reaction force that is
dispatched to help you cope with your threat.

Now for your rapid response team, SWAT team etc. to be
effective, they need resources!

They need uniforms, boots, guns, radios, vehicles, pensions,
unions etc. Your sympathetic nervous System then activates
your Adrenal Cortex which releases the stress hormones that are
required to keep us live under extreme circumstances.

The two main stress hormones which we are going to discuss are
ADRENALIN and CORTISOL.

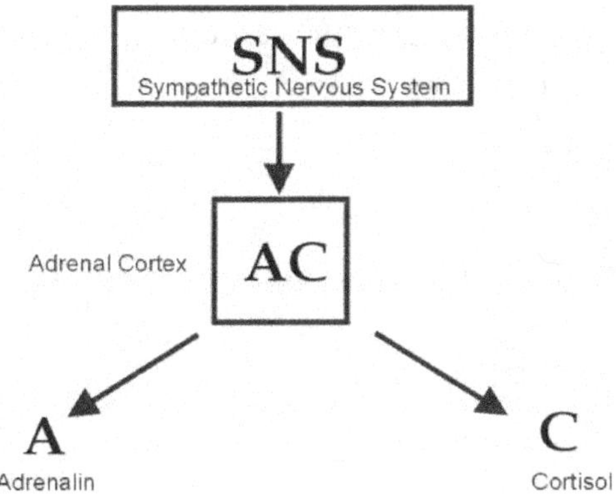

The stress hormones primary function is to conserve and re allocate our bodies resources.

We, as humans, are a closed system – we do not have a power plug and a drip feeding us constantly with energy. Under extreme circumstances, we have whatever resources that are in our system at the time. We therefore need to maximize the efficient us of our resources so that we can survive for the maximum amount of time while fighting or running efficiently.

Adrenalin

Adrenalin has two main functions:

> **Firstly**, Adrenalin locks your Diaphragm. You pant or breathe shallowly. This changes the carbon dioxide,

nitrogen, oxygen mix available to our bodies. This is important for when you are functioning with Cortisol in our systems.

Secondly, Adrenalin pushes your blood pressure up, and keeps it up. You need high blood pressure to direct your resources to where they are needed fast and efficiently. When you are under stress, you need your resources in three places – in your heart lung area, in your big muscles (biceps, triceps, quadriceps and gluteus maximum) for running or fighting, and in your brain.

Adrenalin acts as a vaso-constrictor. It causes muscles and your arteries to constrict. As outlined earlier, the body is a closed system. Within that system you have a fluid filled (blood) distribution network (arteries). If the area of that network is reduced, the laws of hydrodynamics dictate that the pressure has to go up in relation to the reduction of the volume. High blood pressure causes your heart to pump faster, the result being that the resources required by the body while under stress are now being distributed quickly and efficiently.

Adrenalin is not only secreted when you are under stress. There are stimulants that you take which cause the body to release Adrenalin. They are Nicotine – from tobacco products, and caffeine. Caffeine is found in many places, for example;

Soft drinks and sodas, energy drinks, some cold and flu medication, some headache medication, tea, coffee, green tea, diet pills etc. That kick that you get from your morning coffee is an adrenalin rush!

Logic dictates that our stress levels can be moderated to an extent by observing and changing our nicotine and caffeine intake.

Cortisol

Cortisol has five main functions in relation to this explanation.

1. Cortisol helps to **reduce pain and reduce inflammation**. This in effect allows us to function with an injury for a short period of time. In a pre-historic environment, to proto human, Australopithecus, needed to be able to avoid the dangers of the hostile environment in which it lived. If this Australopithecus had twisted its ankle the previous day, today it is hopping around with a swollen ankle. If suddenly it has to evade a predator, it can't afford to hop along, it needs to run and climb fast! Cortisol allows the body to do just that. In the modern world, we have the synthetic form of Cortisol called Cortisone. It is widely prescribed, and I am sure that most readers have taken it at some time. The medical practitioner who prescribes this is normally very specific that when the cortisone has taken effect, we do not exert excessive pressure on the injury. It is important to understand that this medication helps to alleviate the symptoms of a physical trauma so that we can heal in comfort. It does not heal you any faster than your body would normally heal.

2. Cortisol **changes the way our body processes fat**. As most of us know, fat is a wonderfully efficient way for us to store energy, BUT breaking down that fat to release the energy is horribly inefficient. Breaking down fat also releases toxic by-products like ammonia into the body. When you burn fat through physical exercise, significant physiological changes occur. You begin to sweat, trying to cool ourselves and maintain our optimal temperature. You begin to pant or breathe heavily and quickly, you focus specifically on the task at hand and our muscles start to burn. When you are in a life threatening situation – in stress, you cannot afford to experience these side effects. You need the energy to be released from our fat reserves immediately. Cortisol facilitates this for a short period of time. An interesting observation is that you have a fatty deposit (cholesterol) already in our high speed distribution network (our arteries which have reduced in size because of the adrenalin thereby increasing our blood pressure.) This on its own can lead to a negative cardiovascular event, a stroke or a heart attack. Simply put, you have a solvent (Cortisol), a fatty resource (Cholesterol) and a very efficient high pressure distribution system (our arteries). It is inevitable that at some point a solid piece of cholesterol is going to flake off your artery wall and be carried along at high speed to one of the three places where your resources are focused when under stress – the muscles, the heart and the brain.

3. The next three things Cortisol does are **switch off important bodily functions** that use up a lot of energy. Remember that you are a closed system and that the stress reaction in our body forces us to become very efficient. You need to conserve and re allocate the bodies resources. The third thing that Cortisol does is switch off the urge to reproduce. Our sex drive is diminished. Remember that stress is designed for a short intense reaction, so if your sex drive is suspended for a few hours, it does not really have an impact on you, however the long term effects can be devastating.

4. The fourth effect of Cortisol is to **switch off or inhibit your digestion**. It takes up a vast amount of our energy to process and digest our food and manage the resulting waste material. Your stress reaction will cause you to throw up, urinate and void your bowls. It does not sound very nice, but what you are effectively doing is emptying your digestive system from both ends and shutting it down. There is only one way for nutrients to enter your body, and that is through your digestive system. If that system is switched off or its effectiveness reduced as a result of stress, our whole physiology will be put out of balance very quickly. Stress is designed for a short intense reaction, so if your digestion is suspended for a few hours, it does not really have an impact on you, but if it is suspended for twenty years or more, psychological and physiological problems result.

5. The fifth and last thing to be switched off by Cortisol is **cell division**. This is the most important basic bodily function you have. Cell division is how you heal yourself. Every single time that you heal, the healing is a direct result of your cells dividing and replicating. No medication or other therapy can heal you; all they do is help to place your body into an optimal state so that your cells can divide efficiently.

Another important factor that a lot of people do not realize is that you are constantly replicating our selves. Within seven years, every cell in your body had been replaced at least once!

Once again you can see that the short term effects of this stress reaction are negligible, but the long term effects are huge. Stress inhibits our healing and accelerates our ageing!

This concludes the physiological response and the psychology behind our stress response.

What we will do now is use these same responses to effectively manage our stress and to use our stress to enhance our growth and performance.

Chapter Six

Emotional Aspects of Stress

The nature of stress is that it is emotional. Our emotions are a result of hormones being released into our system, and those hormones are usually released to manage a perceived change in our world.

Emotional Maturity

To understand and manage stress a person needs a healthy amount of emotional intelligence. If there is no emotional intelligence there will only ever be responses to external stimuli and never an analysis of behaviour. Without emotional understanding there can be no stress management.

How we feel about something now, can change with time. It is important to understand that feelings are reality are different. How we feel about things can however trigger a secondary stress response. A big wave surfer and a person who is not comfortable with the ocean see the reality of a stormy sea very differently. Both of their feelings are correct in accordance to their world view, but neither change the severity of the storm.

Spirituality and Stress

Spirituality is an area of stress which seems to be in conflict with its self. The essence of spirituality and other more formal and traditional religions is to help an individual to live a good, wholesome and fulfilling life in accordance with the culture within which they have been born.

Spirituality serves to define our position in an uncertain world and it should strengthen our resolve to function well and improve ourselves.

Negative Aspects of Spirituality – Stress Causing

Most people who have been involved in or are currently involved with a religion can relate to feelings of guilt, alienation, fear, inability to perform in accordance to others expectation, overwhelming responsibility for others and feeling powerless or helpless.

Every one of these can cause excessive stress in an individual because the nature of a religion is to curry favour with an omnipotent all powerful being.

If the being is let down or disappointed in any way the love and support bestowed on the individual for being a good person, and there for the very identity of the individual and what they are striving for, can be lost.

This is not specifically limited to religion. Membership of a spiritual group and the possible exclusion from that group causes stress!

The consequences of this perceived loss are usually insurmountable.

Positive Aspects of Spirituality – Stress Diminishing

The intended use of spirituality and religion in a society or culture was to enhance the individual, to motivate them to better themselves and help others. Positive aspects of spirituality and religion are reflected in feelings of faith, courage, feeling positive in the face of adversity, hope, well being and building a sense of strong community.

If these feelings can be consciously cultivated within a religious or spiritual community, great strides will be made to help diminish the feelings of stress and will enhance an individual's well being.

Chapter Seven

Corporate and Work Stress

A corporate environment is sometimes tough!

A group of individual strangers are thrust together to achieve a common goal and in most cases with very little consideration to each person's individuality, abilities and personality. What exacerbates this in a lot of cases is the idea that leadership roles are seen as rewards for good performance rather than roles that need competent leaders!

This is where most of modern stress is experienced. There have been a vast number of studies done on human behaviour and performance in the work place.

The majority of sick days are a result of unmanaged stress or illness resulting from excessive modern stress.

Work and the resulting work stress cannot be avoided. There are however aspects of ourselves and the work environment that we can understand better to reduce and assist in our stress management.

Personality

All human beings are different and they all have different world views. It is vital to try to find work or place employees in areas that interest them, and if this is not possible, at least be consciously aware that the job is not the best fit for the individual and that they will just have to tough it out instead of having to adapt themselves to try and be who they are not and creates stress. "People tend to gravitate towards jobs which fit their personalities; in fact one of the main causes of work stress is lack of fit between the two" (Argyle 66)

It is actually easy to identify what we like. Take a walk through a book shop and take note of the sections that you gravitate towards and where you stop and page through the books. This shows you what you like!

Your answers to three simple questions will guide a person to areas where they will find satisfaction and meaning at work. These are;

What do I want?

What makes me happy?

What excites me?

Combining personality with suitable vocational training and education is a winning formula for beating stress at work. An imbalance here can lead us to other aspects of work stress.

Causes of Work Stress

Michael Argyle outlines nine causes of work stress. All of these are directly related to an inability of the individual to efficiently follow the perception, world, awareness cycle. If there is an interruption in the flow of the cycle, the aspects of perception, world, and awareness drive each other further and further apart negatively exacerbating our stress experience.

The nine causes of work stress where we will experience imbalance are as follows;

> **1. Job Status and satisfaction**. This is usually better in higher paid technical or skill intensive jobs compared to unskilled or middle management jobs. This is because unskilled or (manual labour jobs) and middle management jobs are time and outcome based with little room for error, or there are intense interpersonal interactions that affect time based outcomes. There is also little control over a workers personal space and functions and there needs to be a satisfaction of outcome and a satisfaction of higher authority. Here the

perception of one's self in the world is adversely affected.

2. Job overload is also related to job satisfaction. The work may be too difficult and the time frames for completion too short. "Time pressure is experienced by those on assembly lines, or other kinds of machine paced work, and their health is found to be worse than for other employees" (Argyle 265) Again Perception of the person in the world is affected.

3. Lack of control is directly related to time constraints imposed on work outcomes as well a reduction in autonomy. Industrial manual labour experiences high stress levels because of this. The factors involved here are monotony, time constraints and the lack of control. The awareness of an individual's lack or control and lack of the ability to change the situation is the stressor here.

4. Repetitive work greatly undermines how an individual sees themselves in the world and the perception - world and awareness cycle serves to highlight this repetition and lack of control.

5. Danger "Perceived danger leads to lower levels of performance in most people, but training and experience can prevent this" (Argyle 267) Danger, lack or autonomy and upper management performance demands are a major contributor to post traumatic stress disorder. To unbundle this people should follow the post traumatic stress exercises.

6. Environmental stress. A person's physical environment serves to both relax and motivate a person or it dramatically reduces a person's endurance and resilience. Factors such as noise, heat, cold and even commuting to work are environmental stressors. These types of stressors will engage and exacerbate our modern low level intensity stress and can slowly erode an individual's health and well being.

7. Responsibility for others is a major contributor to stress. If the person in a responsible role does not have the personality to deal with others they will experience high levels of stress. Their perceived ability to cope with other people or be responsible for other people's well being overwhelms them and severe stress responses occur. "Supervisors and managers have worse health than professional workers" (Argyle 268)

8. Role conflict or ambiguous roles results in low job satisfaction. If an individual is constantly unsure of their role they will tend to perform worse and worse as time progresses. This is a result of the memory accumulation cycle that keeps repeating and reinforces the lack of job satisfaction and negativity.

9. Burn out is "a kind of emotional exhaustion and loss of concern for people which is commonly found among those in the medical and helping professions and among administrators who have to deal with a lot of people" (Argyle 269) loss of compassion and the decrease of self worth and motivation are signs of burn out. Intense intervention is required to gain the perception, world and awareness balance.

As best you can Identify some of the nine areas above that you experience in your work environment and start making positive changes to address them within the framework of your personality and the working environment.

Managing Conflict

All interpersonal relationships are based on the Perception, Awareness, World cycle. It is as important to manage conflict effectively in our personal relationships as it is in our work environment.

As such, the main cause of corporate stress is internal and external conflict. "Frustration lies at the core of most conflicts that occur… When individuals in a win-lose mode feel that movement towards their objectives is being blocked or hindered, they can become self centred and disruptive" (Pienaar 188)

This conflict is a direct result of differences in perception. On a personal level, stress in a corporate environment will be a result of differences between people and groups of people. These could be differences in religion, culture, race, language, morals, ethics, social standing, wealth, age, and sex. These differences in perception or world view are easy to manage if we are aware of them and can maturely take others opinions and behaviours into account when we are expressing our self analysis and frustration.

Conflict Prevention

It is vital to pre-empt any stressful confrontations by structuring tasks and commands clearly. The following points may help in reducing unnecessary frustration and conflict.

- Start with the outcome so that all parties are clear as to the goal or expected outcome.

- Define a collective strategy to achieve the outcome.

- Assign specific tasks to group members.

- Highlight time lines for completion of tasks.

- Define a clear reporting and problem solving structure.

- Implement suitable stage monitoring to resolve issues before situations become critical

- Group reward when project completed

These points serve to focus a group on a single common awareness of the world. As the individuals in the group progress through their tasks, they are shifting their perception of themselves usually becoming more confident and competent.

This shift changes the group awareness and the end goals become more and more believable. In essence effective stress management at work involves cultivating group perception, group awareness and celebrating the resulting group achievements.

Again a stress diary being kept by workers and management will highlight issues before they become problems and they can be addresses effectively as they arise. If there is no awareness of the problem, there can be no solution to the problem and it exacerbates its self until open conflict results. Simple corporate stress management tips are listed later in the book.

Chapter Eight

Post Traumatic Stress

Part of the cause of post traumatic stress is the realisation that, and experience of, the horror of a situation that is so far removed from a person's expectation.

This horror has happened in a moment and the confusion and subsequent stress is created by the realisation that it actually happened to you, that you survived and that you now need to deal with what happened.

This horror or confusion can be experienced in situations such as war, natural disasters, and domestic violence and even through social media.

Our memories accumulate so if a person obsessively watches news media and sees war, mayhem, unregulated violence and disasters daily, they can exhibit signs of post traumatic stress.

Part of this problem is that in a lot of extreme violence or trauma cases, the person has had to themselves descend into this abyss of horror and be an active participant of it to be able to extract themselves from the circumstance: a soldier has to fight to survive, a domestic violence victim needs to face their attacker at their level physically or in court, a first responder needs to touch, manage and assist the victims in a horrific accident. In many cases the only way out is to become the malevolence that the victim is most afraid of!

Isolation and Separation from Help

Other aspects of post traumatic stress are varying degrees of separation and self isolation from those who can help.

Often those experiencing the stress are those who had to physically deal with and be involved in the stressful situation. They are then pressurized by authority figures, who were not there in the situation, to provide explanations that match the authoritarian narrative rather than what actually happened.

This forces those experiencing the stress to internalize it and then relate the events in accordance to what authority wants to hear rather than express themselves correctly.

Instead of survival rewards and accolades the participants often feel as if they are ridiculed, scorned or have failed. They fail to acknowledge that they made whatever decisions they made under extreme circumstances and that the fact that they survived is a triumph of immense magnitude!

Taking the memory accumulation cycle into account, when the participants in the stressful event are isolated, they continually internally reassess their experience and as such are compounding the severity of what they have experienced. They isolate themselves more and more and any form of help or therapy can subconsciously be seen as just more of the same authority that they have to explain to. Vital external help can there for be rejected, and is rejected specifically as a way to try and cope with the situation!

Self analysis and peer group sessions are effective ways round this self isolation phenomenon.

Post Traumatic Stress - Self Analysis

To effectively deal with this stress and self isolation, we need to think about our stress, but as you now know, you will re-live our stress when you are thinking about it.

What you therefore want to do it choose a safe time and place where you can go to for half an hour a week to observe and process our stress. This could be your local coffee shop on a weekday afternoon, or your garden on a Sunday. Choose a time and place that suits you and be ready to process your stuff!

If you don't know what the things are that you need to process, look through your general diary. Look for those emotions and thoughts that are in your mind that are out of place and context. An example of this would be thinking of a past motor vehicle accident while you are in a board meeting or writing an exam. This is unusual and needs your attention.

Expanded Motor Coordination

We now use the same writing – motor coordination principal but expand it dramatically.

Once again, writing is a form of exercise and motor co-ordination. Writing is a very complicated set of neural and motor commands and sequences that requires our brains to assign vast amounts of processing power to that task. We there for have less processing power available to focus on whatever is stressing us.

To start to deal with your post traumatic stress you are going to borrow some simple principles from two of the most under rated organizations in our society – the AA (Alcoholics Anonymous) and the NA (Narcotics Anonymous). Their procedure is simplified as follows;

1. Identify a problem

2. Give it importance

3. Go to a meeting

4, Use a sponsor as a safety net

Identify a problem. You use our normal work diary to start to identify our post traumatic stress challenges. You are already forcing your awareness by keeping your work stress diary. You will by now have noticed that certain events in your life are popping into your mind at unusual or inopportune times. These are the events that most probably will be causing some of your post traumatic stress. These are the events that you can start to process as post traumatic stress. You will call this event "E"

Give it importance. It is interesting to note that as soon as you have decided to deal with an issue that has been troubling you, that issue seems to shrink. It is as if it knows that you will be dealing with it in due course and that it does not have to keep on pestering you for attention. Giving a post traumatic stress event importance in your life is the first very important and powerful step to dealing with the event successfully.

Go to a meeting. Figuratively, going to a meeting is the most effective thing you can do to manage your post traumatic stress. You have blocked out a portion of your time in your diary and will only deal with the event in that time. If you are not prepared to allocate a specific time to dealing with your post traumatic stress, then you either have not correctly identified a problem, or you have not given it enough importance. It is easy to allocate time and seriousness to the healing process when there are other members of a group working with you. Prepare the work in your own private time and create a resume of your personal findings for presentation to the support group. This summary should include a basic outline as well as areas where the processing was difficult and easy.

Going to a meeting is the same as joining a group and fulfils important basic needs which a person need fulfilled. These are the "needs for security, status, self-esteem, affiliation, power and goal achievement" (Organizational Behaviour 286)

Use a sponsor as a safety net. For this process our sponsor or safety net will be the written work that is produced during the process. If you have a support group or friends that you can discuss this with it is great, but do not substitute the writing (motor co-ordination) with talking in the group. The discussion, if any, should be supplementary only.

Thinking About the Event

It is important to remember that to deal with post traumatic stress; you need to think about the event. By thinking about the event, you will have an accumulated stress reaction that possibly is more severe than the original survival reaction that you had at the time of the event. You there for need to prepare for this thinking process. It is important that a person find a safe place in their environment - under a tree in the garden, sitting quietly in the bedroom – it does not matter, as long as the place is quiet and makes you feel safe. You then allocate a maximum of 30 minutes to this processing procedure.

When your 30 minutes is over, stop the processing procedure and commit to yourself to return the following week to continue. This process is not to be rushed. It can be as short as two weeks, or as long as six months to a year. The procedure takes as long as it takes for you to find your power and understanding in the event.

The Post Traumatic Stress Processing Procedure

You identify your problem, you give it importance, you go to a meeting, and you call on a sponsor (in this case our sponsor is writing)

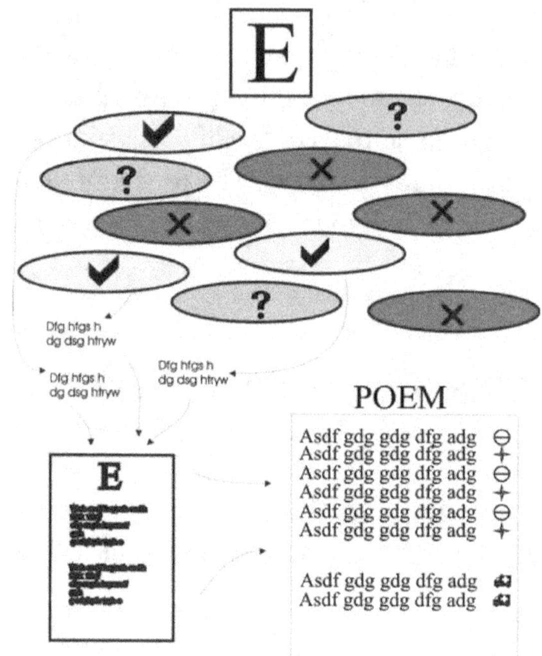

Free Association Words

In your safe place, you write down the title or name of the event (E) and start with free association words relating to the event. You write down as many words as it takes, write down all the single words that describe how you feel about the event.

When your 30 minutes is over, close your book and leave the event alone. Make a commitment to return to the event via the processing procedure in the next scheduled time.

Repeat this procedure until you can honestly not think of any more words that describe your emotional response to the event.

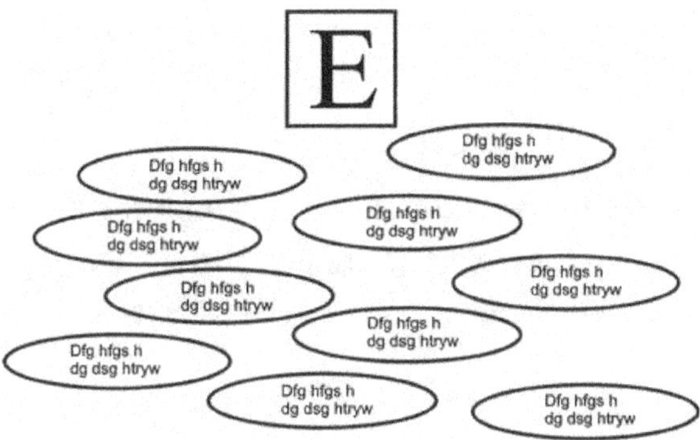

When you have finished writing your words, keep using your allocated time and space to now go back and edit those words.

Editing Words

Ask yourself if these emotive responses are actually what you feel about the event, or are they responses that you think that you should feel about the event.

Our societal and religious enculturation can create huge amounts of secondary stress when the constructs of the society and or the religious beliefs are in conflict with how you actually feel. To process our stress effectively you need to be responsible to yourself first and observe the emotional response for what it is – a primitive survival response. This is a personal journal that you are compiling. No one will be reading it of commenting on it unless you choose to share it with the group. You need to be as honest with yourself as possible.

Once you have empowered yourself through the analysis of the situation, you can then behave and act physically in your world in accordance with the customs of your society and your religion.

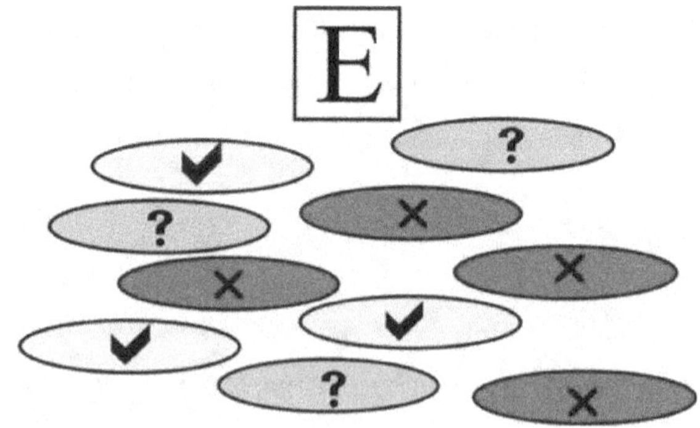

When you have edited your words, you can now start to analyse the words. Look up the meanings of the words in the dictionary. Write two or three line sentences explaining these words to yourself and explaining these words in the context of your event. You need to keep it very simple. Use point form if necessary and use a sponsor as a safety net. When working in a group, let the group members ask if each word is important.

Writing a Letter

The next step is to compile a detailed letter or essay using the sentences that you have derived from the emotive words. Imagine that you are writing this essay or letter for someone on the other side of the world, someone who has no idea who you are and what your social, political and emotional circumstances are. Explain the event as holistically as possible, but do not slip into presupposed societal norms – If you enjoyed or were elated about something that others would find weird, write it down anyway. It is important to be honest with yourself as this is a system that is designed to help you with your stress, not a system that will help you gain favour with or be shamed by others!

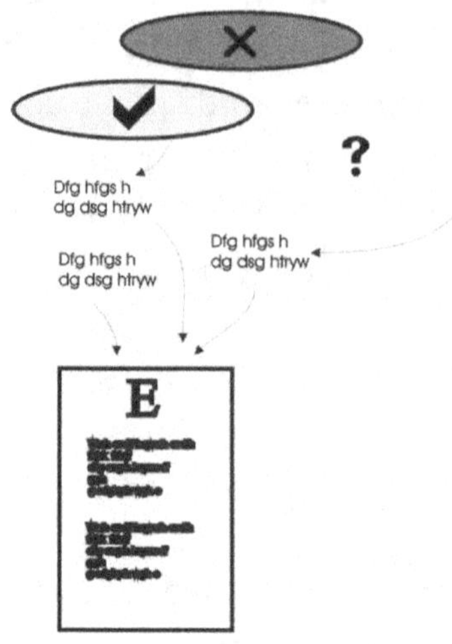

The purpose here is to externalize all the logic, reasoning, reactions, emotions and other linked emotion. It serves to order the thoughts and events in a way that is understandable to the person and by writing the letter by hand, motor co-ordination slows everything down and helps stop the memory accumulation cycle and stops the repeated stress response. This letter needs to be long – three or four pages long...

The awareness of the event is forced to change by the use or syntax and there for the perception of the event changes and the healing process can begin. The letter at this point serves to change both the perception of the traumatic event and the awareness of the event and unlink a lot of the accumulated memories which thereafter have no relevance to the traumatic event.

The perception, awareness and world cycle has been stopped and reversed and you now are in control of how you project your awareness to the world so you can perceive it differently.

Once you have compiled your letter, read through it one more time and then put it away for future reference. You will notice that the event now has taken on new meaning for you.

The event has not been erased; it has been managed to the extent that you have been empowered by the understanding of the event and your response to it.

Your safety net is your diary. If the event is still troubling you write it down in the diary and continue the process. What this process does is stop the perception, world and awareness cycle and possibly reverse it in relation to this specific event.

Understanding your Post Traumatic Stress Emotions

Emotional stress is a unique experience. It is hard for you to identify a single event that triggered the stress response. You therefore need to work on it and take it apart piece by piece to find the truth of your reaction.

You follow the same procedure as you did for general stress and post traumatic stress however you take it one step further.

Trauma Poem

You find an unusual event in your stress diary, write your words, edit your words, write your sentences, and write you essay or letter, and now you convert that letter into a poem.

This may sound strange, but those of you who have read or studied poetry will know how emotive it is. To illustrate this, read a war poem by Siegfried Sassoon, Wilfred Owen or Thomas Hardy.

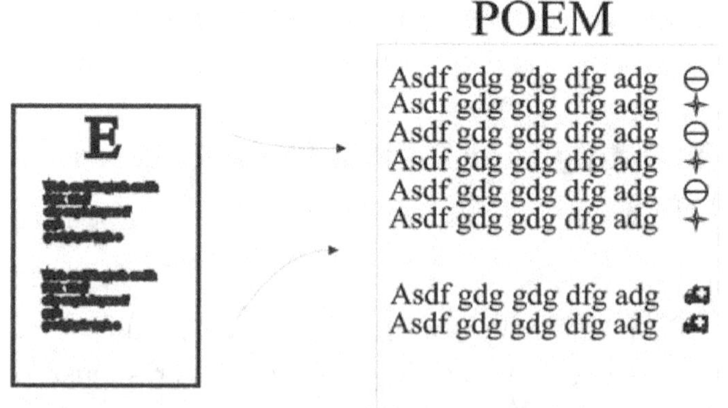

Poetry locks an emotion into a very formal and ridged structure. A sonnet for example is eight to twelve lines long, last word of every second line rhyming. The last two lines are a rhyming couplet.

The process of converting your letter into a poem will force you to understand the actual underlying meaning of the event. The strict format of the poem helps you to understand the emotion and keep it in perspective in relation to you and your life.

It is interesting to note that if you read this poem or other diary entry at a future date you will automatically feel differently about the events they portray and you will naturally want to edit the writing accordingly.

The poetry writing is not a static process but a process that directs the racing or wandering mind to a conclusion that allows you to cope. The subsequent accumulation of memory about the event serves to bring understanding and healing to you because of the event.

Chapter Nine

Simple and Effective Intervention Techniques

The basic causes of stress are an imbalance in our perception and our awareness. Immediate intervention methods will reduce brain speed and modify the Perception, World and Awareness cycle. This will switch the stress response off where necessary and will naturally assist us to adapt to the current circumstances.

The Relaxation Response

The relaxation response is a term Cox uses to describe the physiological stress response when used to switch our stress response off. "As soon as you decide that a situation is no longer dangerous, your brain stops sending emergency signals to your hypothalamus, which in turn ceases to send panic messages to your nervous system. Within about three minutes after the body shuts off the danger signals, the primitive stress response "burns out".

Your metabolism, heart rate, breathing rate, muscle tension and blood pressure all return to their normal levels. You can use your mind to change your physiology for the better, improving your health and perhaps reducing your need for medication.

"The Relaxation Response" refers to this natural restorative process." (Cox 26) The first step in managing our stress requires us to switch off or selectively control our physiological pathway. You can see from the above explanations that to manage our stress you need to first manage the secretion of our stress hormones. Immediate intervention is relatively simple.

To reduce our stress in the moment, we need to break down adrenaline. A vitamin B supplement is effective for this, but an easier and immediately effective way to do this is to breathe.

Breathing

Breathing - The effects of Adrenalin can be managed with oxygen.

Oxygen is a reducing agent – it breaks things down. You paint metallic surfaces to reduce the incidence of rust (oxidization of the iron), you vacuum pack food to keep it fresh for longer, and this effectively removes the oxygen that facilitates the breaking down of the organic matter.

Our muscles are caused to contract by the presence of adrenalin. Oxygen will enable the muscles to relax. I am sure you know how pain full it can be to have a massage! What is happening is your massage therapist is finding those "knots" and squeezing them.

By doing that, the blood that is in the tensed up muscle is forced out into the venous system. There are one way valves in our veins which do not allow the blood to return back to the muscle. You have effectively created a vacuum in that muscle, and when pressure is released, fresh blood will be sucked in from the capillaries, which are connected to the arteries, which come from the heart and lungs.

Arterial blood is rich in oxygen, and it is the presence of this oxygen that allows your muscles to relax. Your arteries are muscles. These muscles have constricted in the presence of Adrenalin and they are keeping your blood pressure up. If you add oxygen, these arteries will relax and dilate thereby reducing your blood pressure.

Lower blood pressure reduces the fuel available to the brain. This reduction in fuel reduces the speed at which the brain can operate and will result in the 25HZ stress trigger being tripped again and the stress response switched off. (Cox 36) To start to manage your stress in the moment, a person just needs to take a deep breath. The oxygen will allow the arteries to dilate and the blood pressure will be reduced.

Any system like Martial Arts, Yoga, Meditation, Chanting, and Singing will teach a person to breathe.

As you learn to be aware of your breathing and practice slowing and normalizing your breaths, your mind will quiet and your body will relax." (Cox 71) Breathing control and techniques can enhance a person's well being and even their emotional state. Breathing and oxygen counter the effects of Adrenalin and can immediately reduce a person's stress! (Cox 71)

The breathing process as follows; During inhalation, air is drawn in through your nose, it is warmed to body temperature as it passes around the turbinate bones in the sinuses, humidified, and partially cleansed. "Your diaphragm, a sheet-like muscle separating the lungs and the abdomen, facilitates your breathing by expanding and contracting as you breathe in and out." (Cox 71) "Your lungs are like a tree with many branches (bronchial tubes) that carry air to elastic air sacks (alveoli)

The alveoli have the balloon like ability to expand when air is taken into the lungs and contracts when air is let out. Small blood vessels (capillaries) surrounding the alveoli receive oxygen and transport it to your heart." (Cox 71) The heart pumps blood around the body specifically to rout blood past the lungs so that CO2 can be released and O2 absorbed. It is the haemoglobin of the red blood corpuscles that holds the O2.

This is very efficient as large amounts of blood can be processed in a short space of time. (Cox 71) When you breathe, you typically use one of two patterns:

    1.Chest or Thoracic breathing.

2. Abdominal or diaphragmatic breathing.

Chest or thoracic breathing is usually a sign of anxiety or other emotional distress. Chest breathing is shallow, irregular and rapid. When air is inhaled, the chest expands and the shoulders rise to take in the air. Anxious people (people in prolonged modern stress) may experience breath holding, hyperventilation or constricted breathing, shortness of breath, or fear of passing out.

If an insufficient amount of air reaches your lungs, your blood is not properly oxygenated, your heart rate and muscle tension increase, and your stress reaction will automatically turn on. There is something restricting normal breathing that needs attention!

This stress response within a stress response will dramatically exacerbate the negative effects of a person's stress. (Cox 72) "Abdominal or diaphragmatic breathing is the natural breathing of newborn babies and sleeping adults. Inhaled air is drawn deep into the lungs and exhaled as the diaphragm contracts and expands. Breathing is even and non-constricting." (Cox 72) As Cox mentioned earlier, by increasing your awareness of your own breathing patterns and practising breathing exercises, you can reduce the muscle tension and anxiety present with stress related symptoms or thoughts.

Diaphragmatic breathing is the easiest way of engaging the relaxation response. (Cox 72) I use a simple and easy breathing technique when I am cold and again when I am rock climbing and need to quickly refresh myself and reduce cramp. I found this technique in Lobsang Rampa's book Doctor from Lhasa.

This simple technique has been the foundation of my spiritual exploration for the last twenty years! To perform this breathing technique, draw in a deep breath through the nostrils, then exhale all of the air in three equally spaced sharp out breaths through the mouth.

These out breaths should be performed as if you are blowing out candles but with more vigour and at the end of the third breath as much air as possible should have been exhaled form the lungs.

Imagination and Controlling Awareness

To manage Cortisol effectively, you need to manage your 25 Hz switch. To manage your switch, you need to manage your imagination, and to manage your imagination, you need to be in touch and directing your perception and awareness.

This is the fundamental purpose of all spirituality, religion, and other self help or motivational systems!

The main thrust of this it to consciously observe out internal dialogue and to direct that dialogue to positive rather than negative outcomes.

I have observed in myself that I spend over 3 hours a day conducting arguments in my head - arguments with people who are not in front of me or who are not even aware of my frustration with them!

Remember that every time we imagine ourselves in conflict, our bodies are reacting physically as if we are physically in conflict, and these imaginary conflicts exacerbate out negative memory accumulation cycle there by exacerbating our physical and emotional stress.

To manage this internal conflict we need to consciously be aware of our subconscious activity. To cultivate this awareness all we need to do is write things down! Writing with a pen on paper is important because writing is a complicated motor co-ordination process.

As discussed earlier, motor coordination overrules our stress reaction. Just as the subconscious does not differentiate between real and imagined events, so to, any form of motor coordination will draw our cerebral cortex resources away from thinking and assign those resources to controlling the body.

Meditation

An active meditation where one finds a peaceful centre and then undertakes an examination of our world view, our perception of ourselves in the world, how we see ourselves in relation to others and or systems and then exploring various outcomes to the situation that we would like to experience. This will both make positive outcomes believable as well and allow us to examine the steps need to be taken to achieve those outcomes. This serves to make the desired outcomes believable and naturally boosts our self worth.

Another aspect of meditation is the fact that the racing mind which is tripping the stress trigger is allowed to slow down and various breathing techniques that are sometimes employed as preparation to meditation will naturally lower bold pressure, oxygenate the system and slow the brain down!

Mindfulness

Mindfulness is a state of suspended animation where all the inputs from our world are assessed and categorized without judgement in the present moment and then scheduled for proper attention by us at an appropriate time. The idea is to live in the present moment with no expectation or reference points from the past to force a person into an inappropriate assessment of the moment. Mindfulness is a wonderful state of mind that is calm and peaceful. It requires time, practice and dedication to achieve and maintain.

Conscious Awareness

Conscious awareness is a form of introspection awareness where the individual mind becomes aware of its self.

To do this the mind needs to be aware of sensory experiences in the body and simultaneously be aware of where these sensory experiences came from – all in the same moment. If an individual can achieve this they will effectively recreate heir perception, world and awareness cycle for every experience.

Stress creation and memory accumulation would be suspended and the body would either begin to recover or would not experience stress.

Education

Preparation for stress- The most logical way to manage stress is to prepare ourselves for it. If we are prepared for a situation, we will be able to sustain an effective and efficient response over time without the negative aspects of stress. Preparation requires a shift in consciousness which makes the idea of coping with the stressful situation believable. If it is believable in our subconscious mind, we can physically cope and thrive. Undergoing initiation, being educated and making simple lifestyle changes will prevent a large portion of our stress from occurring at all!

Education prepares you for a stressful encounter. The point of education is to allow an organism to become proficient in a specific field so that that organism can operate proficiently in a stressful environment where that learned skill set is required. A lawyer studies law so that they can be proficient in law and perform well in that environment. A soldier undergoes rigorous training to enable him or her to cope in a specific military situation.

Education is the fundamental key to preparing one's self for stress, and "the more you know about a topic, the easier it is to absorb further new information about it" (Cohen 53). As such stress when consciously applied and used can and will enhance our knowledge and performance.

Initiation

Initiation is probably the most powerful tool that humans can use to prepare themselves to manage stress and adversity. An initiation is a kind of emotional and spiritual vaccine. It serves to force the shift in consciousness by putting people in symbolic situations "where consciousness and spiritual maturity can grow rapidly." (Marlantes 9)

Initiation serves to mark a transition from one level of consciousness and responsibility to another and is used consciously and unconsciously all the time. Traditional or ancient cultures had rites of passage, societies and groups have an entrance test or requirement to be attained before entry, societies and institutions have advancement badges or stages that its members pass though, even corporations instil in their new workers a corporate identity (shirts, branded merchandise, even business cards) and there is some form of group identity that is either formally or informally required for members – even going to a bar for drinks with work colleges is a form of initiation and serves to create an identity and sense of belonging to the group.

"Joseph Henderson, a world authority on initiations… explained that here are two broad categories of initiation experiences. The first kind prepares the individual to fulfil an adult role in his or her society. Traditionally it was where the boys learned to accept the danger and responsibility involved in hunting and the girls learned to accept the danger and responsibility involved in childbirth. The second kind goes beyond societal roles and is of a spiritual nature. It is about accepting ones mortality. It is about facing death." (Marlantes 9)

Initiation sounds complicated however it is actually simple. If you are going on a journey, you prepare yourself for that journey. If you are in the military, you go through basic and specialist training to emotionally and physically mature you to cope with the circumstances that you may encounter. If you are entering a specific career, you educate yourself to be able to be proficient in the aspects of maturity and cognitive skills that will enable you to perform well in that career environment. If for example an accountant suddenly has to be a first responder or specialist surgeon, their stress levels would elevate dramatically as they are not prepared to manage the situation, nor have they confidence or emotional maturity to cope with the situation forced upon them.

All of these immediate interventions are very common and make up the normal social experience of most humans. Being more aware of them and applying them consciously in our lives will dramatically reduce our experience of stress.

Chapter Ten

Self Assessment Activities

Stress is an incredibly personal experience. It is important to honestly assess yourself. There are things in your life known only to you and you need to be honest with yourself and allow these private experience become part of your assessments and healing.

There are three simple methods that I have used for this book. These are easy ways for readers to assess their stress and identify areas that they can work on to manage their stress. These methods also help to create awareness of stressful areas in a person's daily life and promote intervention before the negative aspects of the stress become too severe.

The Simple Stress Audit

To help people better understand their responses to things and to assess where their main stress comes from, I have developed and regularly use a simple stress assessment questionnaire.

This questionnaire is to be used and assessed in two ways

Firstly, the accumulative numbers responses will quickly show a user how stressed they are at that moment in time.

Secondly, the questions with the highest numerical answers will then show the user what areas of their lives are causing them the most stress.

It must be noted that this questionnaire and the results there of is a general guideline starting point. The stress response is very fluid and detailed results of this assessment can change dramatically over time. Please use this assessment questionnaire as often as you like to help you keep on top of your stress!

Conducting The Stress Audit

Circle the number that represents your emotional involvement in each area, 1 being the least involved and 10 being maximum level of involvement. (Cox 56)

Bought, Sold or Moved House 1 2 3 4 5 6 7 8 9 10

Major House Renovation 1 2 3 4 5 6 7 8 9 10

Separation from a loved one 1 2 3 4 5 6 7 8 9 10

End of relationship 1 2 3 4 5 6 7 8 9 10

Got engaged 1 2 3 4 5 6 7 8 9 10

Got married 1 2 3 4 5 6 7 8 9 10

Marital problem 1 2 3 4 5 6 7 8 9 10

Awaiting divorce 1 2 3 4 5 6 7 8 9 10

Divorce 1 2 3 4 5 6 7 8 9 10

Child started school/preschool 1 2 3 4 5 6 7 8 9 10

Increased nursing responsibilities

For elderly or sick person 1 2 3 4 5 6 7 8 9 10

Problems with relatives 1 2 3 4 5 6 7 8 9 10

Problems with friends/neighbours 1 2 3 4 5 6 7 8 9 10

Pet-related problems 1 2 3 4 5 6 7 8 9 10

Work related problems 1 2 3 4 5 6 7 8 9 10

Change in nature of work 1 2 3 4 5 6 7 8 9 10

Threat of redundancy 1 2 3 4 5 6 7 8 9 10

Changed job 1 2 3 4 5 6 7 8 9 10

Made redundant 1 2 3 4 5 6 7 8 9 10

Unemployed 1 2 3 4 5 6 7 8 9 10

Retired 1 2 3 4 5 6 7 8 9 10

Increased loan or house bond 1 2 3 4 5 6 7 8 9 10

Financial difficulty 1 2 3 4 5 6 7 8 9 10

Insurance problem 1 2 3 4 5 6 7 8 9 10

Legal problem 1 2 3 4 5 6 7 8 9 10

Emotional or physical illness of close

Family or relative 1 2 3 4 5 6 7 8 9 10

Emotional or physical illness of

yourself 1 2 3 4 5 6 7 8 9 10

Serious illness of close family or

Relative requiring hospitalization 1 2 3 4 5 6 7 8 9 10

Serious illness requiring your own

Hospitalization 1 2 3 4 5 6 7 8 9 10

Surgical operation on yourself 1 2 3 4 5 6 7 8 9 10

Death of husband of wife 1 2 3 4 5 6 7 8 9 10

Death of family member or relative 1 2 3 4 5 6 7 8 9 10

Death of close friend 1 2 3 4 5 6 7 8 9 10

Birth of grandchild 1 2 3 4 5 6 7 8 9 1

Difficult relationship with children 1 2 3 4 5 6 7 8 9 10

Difficult relationship with parents 1 2 3 4 5 6 7 8 9 10

1_____________________180_________________360

The Target of Change

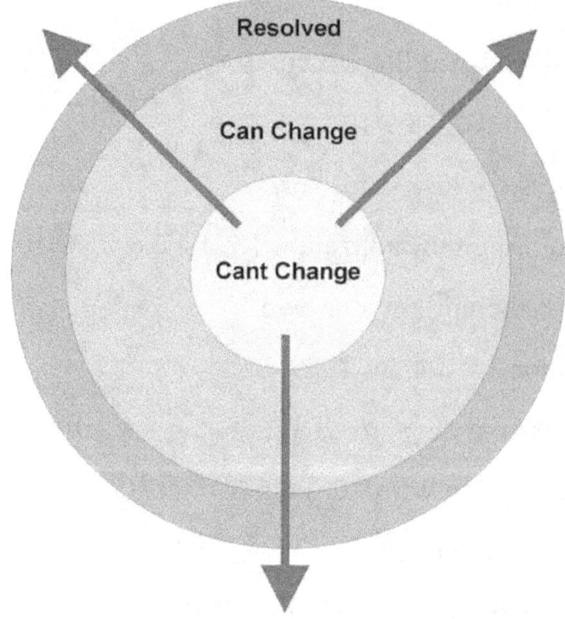

This assessment can follow on from the Simple Stress Audit, where all the high score items or high stress items are placed in the centre of the target, the middle score items or medium stress items in the next ring and the low score items or low stress items in the outer ring.

This target of change can also be used as a standalone system, just list the issues that you have identified in the order of severity from the worst to the least and place them in their respective rings.

Take ONE item or issue at a time as work on resolving the issue until the item can be moved to the next less severe ring.

The Stress Diary

An old fashioned physical book diary is an incredibly useful stress management tool. Physical writing as we will discuss later is a vital stress management tool which you will use often.

By writing down on paper what is going on in your head, you will begin to see a correlation between parts of the day that are more stressful than others. In addition it also becomes possible to see the correlation between types of stressful events and characteristic physical and emotional symptoms you might experience.

The most important part of keeping a diary is that it will help you to start to see exactly who it is or what it is that is bothering you.

By putting these down on paper you give yourself the opportunity to examine the issues properly and clearly and to begin to see them for what they truly are, as well as the real extent of every body's involvement in the actual issue.

The Stress diary allows you to discover and chart your stressful events and the resultant characteristic reactions. For example interpersonal confrontations may result in stomach tension whilst rushing or stuck in queues may result in irritability. Using your body awareness exercises, which is explained later in the book, now allows you to recognize where your body shares its tension.

Allowing yourself increased awareness to note the areas of muscular tension gives you the opportunity to apply a relaxation skill to let go the tension you have discovered. With the release of tension you will experience an increase in your energy level as well as a greater sense of well being.

The diary will help you to identify events that are in your head that need to be sorted out. The persistent and constant communication that goes on in your head, with people who are not present and yet are involved in internal debate and dialogue, points us in the direction of issues that need to be resolved.

Once identified the particular issue is written out and the following formula is applied to the particular situation under review.

How much of this situation is **REAL?**

How much of this situation is **SPECULATION?**

How much of this situation is **IMAGINATION?**

What is important for me to attend to **IMMEDIATELY?**

What can be attended to at a **LATER DATE?**

Once this formula has been worked out, and the issues at hand have been clearly identified, specific decisive action can be taken to address immediate important issues and others can be scheduled for a later date.

You can also use your stress awareness diary to help you to record your progress with the relaxation techniques presented.

Chapter Eleven

Tips for Work, Home and Relationship Stress

Quick tips for beating stress at work

Prioritise– Divide tasks into four categories, in order of priority ranging from "urgent" to "can wait". Make a plan at the start of each day, or even better, at the end of the previous day – stick to it. The more you do it, the quicker you get.

Communicate Assertively– Use these two techniques to handle conflict in the office. The "broken record" method involves stating your case in a calm and clear manner over and over again, ignoring provocation. That doesn't mean you ignore the person you disagree with, but simply stick to your guns without raising your voice. Strategy two is to ask your accuser pointed questions – an effective defence technique which helps you to distinguish between the real mistakes you have made from general criticism thrown at you.

Build Confidence by Being Prepared– You should not expect to be confident about performing a task if you are not prepared and have not practised. It is like taking your driving test without any lessons. Face your fears and become confident through practice and repetition.

Don't go to work if you are ill– You will make yourself more ill when you push yourself to the limit. Despite the culture of "I must be in the office", which is motivated by the fear of losing your job, chances are your colleagues will resent your bringing germs into the office rather than say "well done" . Common colds are a part of life but continuous illness can be a result of stress. A day off to recover can make you more efficient.

Learn to manage your time effectively– Allow time for the unexpected. Avoid procrastination it will not get easier if you delay the task. Process one task at a time. Open incoming mail and deal with It, dump it, or delegate it. Give and demand clear instructions

Vary your routine– Too much routine will manifest boredom and result in stress. If your job is routine defined, work out in advance when you can take a break from certain tasks and switch to others also introduce short relaxation periods.

Deal with criticism objectively– do not immediately over react. Take a deep breath, relax shoulders, and unclench fists. Listen carefully and clarify by repeating the criticism. Ask yourself is this criticism justified in whole or in part. Admit which portion of blame is yours if any, and detail how to rectify it. If no blame is yours state this calmly and clearly.

Expect the Unexpected– Make sure a colleague knows where important information is kept in case you are not present – keep them regularly updated on all events so they can defuse a crisis on your behalf.

A clear desk makes for a clear head– A desk cluttered with things to do like unanswered mail, is a constant reminder of too many things to do and not enough time to do them in. You are also wasting time trying to "find" things.

Have stress free relationships with your colleagues- Accept and deal with your fair share of the workload. Respect others privacy. Be co-operative over shared space. Keep confidences.

Have stress free relationships with your superiors– Always ask if instructions are not clear to you. Use your initiative. Be willing and cheerful. Ask for feedback. Do not be submissive.

Have stress free relationships with your subordinates– Keep them informed of decisions that will affect them. Fight for their interests. Give praise where it is due. Advise and encourage them. Consider their personal problems.

Appropriate responses to actual incidence– Low frustration tolerance is handled by changing the thought of "I can't stand it" or similar. Instead they should tell themselves "I can stand it. I've handled it before and I can handle it again".

Take the tension out of commuting to work– Do not drive aggressively yourself. Make allowances for bad drivers they will not improve by your shouting at them. Try to leave home problems at home and never drive after an argument. Eat a healthy breakfast before leaving home, low blood sugar affects your ability to concentrate.

Quick tips for beating stress at home

Change your approach to housework– Use your time-management techniques from work, train your family to assist. Draw up a roster and stick to it. It's easier than you think.

Throw things away– Be merciless with your own stuff if you have not used it for a year, assess if it is really needed, give it away or throw it away. Make "homes" for all the "where is" stuff, such as sellotape, scissors, keys etc. Everyone must know where it belongs and must return it there.

Combine boring tasks with mental stimulation– Listen to an audio book while doing the ironing!

Reduce electro-magnetic stress– It has been proven that electromagnetic signals from electronic equipment can lead to fatigue, nervous tension, headaches and insomnia. Air rooms by opening windows for at least half an hour every day (even in winter). Use ionisers to counteract positive ions generated by electronic equipment, or use a bowl of water in each room. Sit at least six feet away from the television and remove electrical

gadgets such as clock radios and television sets from your
bedroom.

Practice personal relaxation exercises– Once an expert you can
relax anywhere, but to begin practice in a quiet room for 15 to
20 minutes every day. Use progressive muscle relaxation, tense
and release all muscles in turn from feet to head. Feel the
sensation of tense and relaxed.

Listen to soothing music and not the news– Listen to uplifting
music in the morning; the news will make you feel stressed. The
ideal tempo for relaxation is a bit slower than your heartbeat.

Keep a journal of stressful events– This is great for those who
do not open up or do not want to burden others. The release will
improve your immune system. Writing forces you to define your
emotions and reactions.

See the funny side of things– Laugh Out Loud, even if it's not
that funny. Hearty laughter boosts the production of
immunoglobulin A, which fights viruses. Smiling relaxes
muscles and triggers the production of endorphins, resulting in a
natural high. If you force yourself to smile, you will create a
mood of happiness.

Make meal times stress-free– Eating together should be pleasant
and happy, allowing the family to laugh and exchange stories of
their day. Make the effort to co-ordinate as many meals as
possible for family gathering. Make washing up a fun joint

family venture. Enjoy a romantic candle lit dinner with your partner at least twice a month.

Take time out from work on the weekends– Some people use the weekend to catch up on little jobs that were left during the week, instead of relaxing, sometimes this is unavoidable, but make chore free weekends the rule, rather than the exception.

Quick tips to de-stress your relationships

You cannot change another person; you can only change your responses to that other person.

Once you have agreed to speak about conflict

Be calm.

Be specific.

No speaking in code.

Suggest solutions.

Listen and take notes - taking notes stops us responding to the first few words we hear and allows an explanation to be presented in full.

Remember you are on the same side– The goal of any disagreement is to find a solution that works for both of you, not merely to win or dominate.

Deal with the present problem– Do not drag your last relationship issues into this discussion.

Don't take each other for granted– Respect and honour your partner and yourself in the relationship (Cox 103).

Spend quality time together– Book a date with your partner or friends and stick to it, this can be as fancy or as simple as you like, the point is to connect in person. (Cox 103)

Show affection– Massage each other, Hold hands, touch, hug, kiss, and enjoy each other. (Cox 103)

Sex is a great stress buster, don't misuse it– Sexual issues are usually the symptom of a much larger problem so discuss it. (Cox 103)

"Time Out" during all heated conflicts– If possible – discuss differences of opinion before they turn into conflicts, These discussions should be no longer an 30 minutes and if things are heated, take time out and deal with things again later. (Cox 103)

Learn to respect and demand personal space– You are an individual and need your space – don't be shy to ask for it and to give it when asked.

CONCLUSION

I hope that by now, and the end of this book that you are not more stressed about your stress!

Our life stressors are sometimes well hidden in our daily lives and spiritual belief systems, and have become accepted as what our life is about. By stopping our lives for a moment and changing the way we perceive things, our whole world view shifts, we can never go back to the same way of responding to the world so we have to change.

Stress and our stress responses are very personal and there is no generic quick fix system. Our stress responses changes when our lives change. It is up to the individual to use these methods to assist them to become stress aware and to stress less.

Using the Perception – World – Awareness system outlined in the book we can take charge of our thoughts and our lives. This system is as relevant to stress management as it is to conflict resolution, mediation and metaphysics. Understanding our perception and awareness is an exploration of our own consciousness, an exploration of our culture and society and it shows us where we can explore, grow and enhance our lives.

I hope this unique simple and safe system has a positive impact on everyone in their pursuit of knowledge, insight and happiness in life.

BIBLIOGRAPHY

• Anastasi A, Urbina S, Psychological Testing, Prentice-Hall Inc, 1997, Print

• Argyle M, The Social Psychology of Work, Penguin Books, 1989, Print

• Braden G, The Isaiah Effect, Hay House UK Ltd, 2004, Print

• Buzan T, Use Your Memory, BBC Books, BBC World Wide Publishing, 1997, Print

• Cohen G, Eysenck M W, LeVoi M E. Memory a Cognitive Approach, Open University Press, UK, 1988, Print

• Collins Paperback English Dictionary, Harper Collins, 1991, Print

• Cox C, Stress Management – Powerful solutions for Busy People. Woad Stress Management CC, 2009, EPub

• Cheryl K, Stress & Brain Waves, Sat, 2009-10-31 16:06 http://americannutritionassociation.org/node/257

• Dr Weil A, Eating Well for Optimum Health, Little Brown and Company UK (Warner Books), 2001, Print

• Heindel M, Ancient and Modern Initiation, L N Fowler & Co Ltd 1931, Print

• Hubbard L R, Self Analysis, New Era Publications International APS, Denmark, 2007, Print

• https://en.wikipedia.org/wiki/Walter_Bradford_Cannon

• https://www.stress.org/about/hans-selye-birth-of-stress

• Kiyosaki R, 8 Lessons in Military Leadership, Plata Publishing LLC, 2015, Print

• Marlantes K, What it is Like to go to War, Corvos – Atlantic Books Ltd, 2012, Print

• McCormick E, Ilgen D, Industrial Psychology, George Allen & Unwin London, 1980, Print

• McFadyen I, Mindwars The Battle for your Brain, Allen & Unwin, Australia, 2000, Print

• Newton M, Life Between Lives, Liewellyn Publications, MN 2011, Print

• Osho, Awareness The Key to Living in Balance, St Martins Griffin, NY, 2001, Print

• Papalia D E, Wendkos-Olds S, Psychology, Mc Graw-Hill, 1998, Print

• Pienaar W, Spoelstra M, Negotiation, Theories, Strategies & Skills, Juta & Co Ltd, 1996, Print

• Rampa L, Doctor from Lhasa, Transworld Publishers Ltd (Corgi Books), London, 1968, Print

• Robbins S, Organizational Behaviour, Prentice-Hall Inc 1993, Print

• Runton P T, The Key of Masonic Initiation, John M Watkins, London 1942, Print

9 798714 383441